Lewis Lavoie's

MURAL IN-A BOOK MOSAIC

HUNDREDS OF PAINTINGS — ONE MASTERPIECE MURAL

KUNAMOKST

KUNAMOKST *Coastal Inspirations*

Designed by Lewis Lavoie and created by over 180 coastal artists

Over 180 artists participated by painting a westcoast theme. Each artist was given a 12" x 12" panel with simple guidelines and color tones that they had to consider within their painting. When assembled, it created an incredible 12' x 21' unified mural.

Phil Alain, Paul Lavoie and Lewis Lavoie pose in front of the mural while on display at the 2010 Winter Olympics, Vancouver, Canada

The Mural Mosaic team wishes to thank all participating artists of this project

A special thanks to The Galiano Oceanfront Inn and Spa. (see panel 230)

Kunamokst, Coastal Inspiration © 2009 Mural Mosaic
http://www.muralmosaic.com

Patent Pending

ISBN 978-0-9731896-2-9

Printed and bound in China

FSC
SGS-COC-2659

Mixed Sources
Product group from well-managed forests, controlled sources and recycled wood or fiber
www.fsc.org
© 1996 Forest Stewardship Council

Before & Afters

Without knowing the end result each artist was given the challenge to transform a canvas of shapes and colors into an individual painting.

Panel #156 before...

Panel #218 before...

Panel #143 before...

Panel #156 completed by artist Rohana Laing

Panel #218 completed by artist Mark Hobson

Panel #143 completed by artist James Koll

Please visit **www.muralmosaic.com** to see more and read the comments each artist has written about their piece.

KUNAMOKST
COASTAL INSPIRATIONS

artists list see back page inlet

layout grid see front page inlet

instructions see back pages

more instructions including video see www.muralmosaic.com

Visions Of Haida Gwaii

Inspired from photos I took from the seaplane one summer of clear cuts and the island off Skiddagate.

1

Artist: Judy Baca,   www.judybaca.com
Panel #1
Title: Visions Of Haida Gwaii
Medium: Acrylic

The Overseer 2

As I visited this particular beach I was reminded of the times prior to this industrial devastation. I could not help but wonder what the Haida elders must feel when witnessing the rape of their ancestral lands. It was during this reflection that the idea of placing the totem among the dead driftwood was born. It was like a headstone in a graveyard! After spending some time on the beach, as I started the car a news bulletin came on the radio announcing the death of Bill Reid. It was at that moment that the inspiration for "The Overseer" was born.

2

Artist: Gerald Marchand, www3.telus.net/gmarchand
Panel #2
Title: The Overseer 2
Medium: Acrylic

Panel #003   by Jennie Brickwood

Tako

3

Artist: Jennie Brickwood, www.rockwoodart.com
Panel #3
Title: Tako
Medium: rocks, shells, sea glass in cement

Panel #005 by Lynn Kingham

Beached

5

Artist: Lynn Kingham, www.members.shaw.ca/lkingham
Panel #5
Title: Beached
Medium: Acrylic

This Is My Father's World

I love nature! We planted a Sumac tree when we moved to Burnaby, B.C. from Edmonton. This "burning bush" spreads rapidly by very long shallow running roots and has brilliant autumn foliage.

Our provincial bird is the Stellar Jay. They are very fond of peanuts; if you start feeding them they'll soon wake you up too early with their raucous calls.

Orcas are the largest members of the dolphin family. A few years back I had gone whale watching. Being a dental assistant I was fascinated and also sad to discover that dental abscesses are one of the main causes of death in wild whales.

6

Artist: Lucyna Eschner
Panel #6
Title: This Is My Father's World
Medium: Acrylic

by Huguette Benger

Galiano Sail By

8

Artist: Huguette Benger
Panel #8
Title: Galiano Sail By
Medium: Acrylic

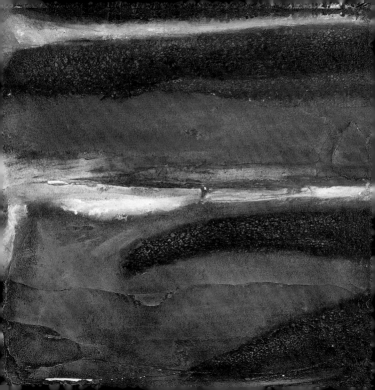

by Catherine Tableau

Dies Irae (Sunset on Marina Island

Electric colors, violence, passion, anger inhabit "Dies Irae". You don't know where starts the sky, where ends the mountains and the seashore but you can feel the storm blowing from this sunset at Shark Spit on Marina Island, B.C..

Dies Irae, irradié, jour de colère, day of anger, end of day, end of a world...

9

Artist: Catherine Tableau, www.catherinetableau.com
Panel #9
Title: Dies Irae (Sunset on Marina Island)
Medium: Plaster on board with acrylic paints

Coastal Motif

10

Artist: Rod Charlesworth, www.rodcharlesworth.com
Panel #10
Title: Coastal Motif
Medium: Acrylic

Journey by Water

Just as my panel is one part of a greater image, so is water. To me, water is the truth and harmony that runs through nature. After the long drop at the top of Shannon Falls, runs the water, that I have painted. It flows, spontaneously yielding and humble on its journey to be a part of something much greater.

11

Artist: Kathy Johnston, www.kathyjohnston.ca
Panel #11
Title: Journey by Water
Medium: Acrylic

Panel #012   by Tim Fraser

Island behind the Maples

12

Artist: Tim Fraser, www.timfraser.ca
Panel #12
Title: Island behind the Maples
Medium: Oil

Gulf Blush

I've been going to Galiano Island since 1973, when we built a family cottage and fell in love with everything about the island, from the beauty of its sandstone shoreline to its laid-back lifestyle. The title of the panel, "Gulf Blush", refers to the glow of a warm summer afternoon's sun on the sculpted sandstone rocks near our island getaway.

13

Artist: Perry Haddock, www.perryhaddock.com
Panel #13
Title: Gulf Blush
Medium: Acrylic

Wreck Diving

Scuba diving has always intrigued me. I worked with someone who went diving every weekend and came back with many adventure stories and amazing photos. Some of the best photos were from shipwreck dives along the coast of Vancouver Island.

It's not surprising that BC is named one of the World's Best Wreck Dive Sites.

14

Artist: Heather Brewster, www.heatherbrewster.com
Panel #14
Title: Wreck Diving
Medium: mixed medium

Panel #015 by Allen Klatt

Looking Westward

A view of Vancouver's North Shore mountains as seen from Sunset Beach in Vancouver. Simular views of sky, mountains, sea and sand can be seen at unnumerable locations on the west coast yet each one is unique and special.

15

Artist: Allen Klatt, www.allenklatt.page.tl
Panel #15
Title: Looking Westward
Medium: Acrylic

The Fabric of Community

Many ethnicities make up the tapestry of society. While we celebrate our differences this colourful version of the flag of British Columbia symbolizes that we are united as one community under the flag.

16

Artist: Barbara Would Schaefer,
Panel #16
Title: The Fabric of Community
Medium: Acrylic

Panel #017   by Kia Hardy

Damp

17

Artist: Kia Hardy, www.kiahardy.weebly.com
Panel #17
Title: Damp
Medium: Acrylic

Sustenance

This image is a close up of the salmon in the mouth of the Raven. Salmon is considered the staple food of many coastal communities, brought to the rivers and seas by the Raven. Legends tell of how Raven stole the salmon from the Beaver people by rolling up their stream and landscape like a carpet and flying away. It was so heavy that he could only fly a short distance at a time. He would stop wherever there was a tree to rest. The Beaver people, in order to stop him, would gnaw down the trees that Raven stopped at and each time some Salmon and stream would escape forming great streams and rivers of Salmon.

18

Artist: Todd Jason Baker, www.nativeonline.com
Panel #18
Title: Sustenance
Medium: Acrylic

Unity

The Cougar and the Bald Eagle are both dominant predators of the West Coast region, therefore I wanted to unite both animals in an acrylic rendering of a West Coast skyline

19

Artist: Jessica Albert,
Panel #19
Title: Unity
Medium: Acrylic

Panel #020   by Maria Miranda Lawrence

Into the Sunset - Long Beach

My panel suggested a sunset scene over a beach. I referenced a photograph I took of my daughter Corinna and her partner Hans-Christen Andersen walking ahead along our island's largest beach.

Merging the two images together, the resulting painting not only captures a memorable moment in time but it foreshadows the warmth and happiness of their long-lasting relationship, as they journey through life together. The original photograph was taken on Vancouver Island's Long Beach, known for its magnificent and expansive natural shoreline by the Grand Pacific Ocean.

20

Artist: Maria Miranda Lawrence, www.mirandalawrence.com
Panel #20
Title: Into the Sunset - Long Beach
Medium: Acrylic

Panel #021   by Ena Hoole

Trincomali Sunset

21

Artist: Ena Hoole
Panel #21
Title: Trincomali Sunset
Medium: Acrylic

Dogwood and the Lunar Moth

I am an artist from the interior of B.C., and in the summer of 2006 had the opportunity to sail and kayak the B.C. coast for five months.
I loved living with the pulse of ocean, moon, and tides. It was while hiking on Calvert Island that I stumbled for my first and only time, across a very pretty, cool patch of blooming dogwood and that inspired my painting.

22

Artist: Lynn Erin, www.fireweedart.ca
Panel #22
Title: Dogwood and the Lunar Moth
Medium: Acrylic

Erin 2009

Thing of Beauty

The ugly and the beautiful Ling Cod. Big and unnerving when you see them live but as you look closer they have the most incredible colours and designs. So many of us have no idea of the diverse and beautiful world just below the water. We spend so much time looking at the vast surface that we never really contemplate that complex underworld. One of my goals is to remove that boundary of air and water and have the viewer consider that space which is often just below our vision.

23

Artist: Kenna Fair, www.kennafair.com
Panel #23
Title: Thing of Beauty
Medium: Oil on carved wood

Panel #024   by Carla Maskall

West Coast Spawning Salmon

West Coast nature is one of the most inspirational and beautiful muses for an artist. Nature becomes a central theme in most of my works these days as I see the fragile beauty of it threatened by our misuse. In our busy world, my goal as an artist is to give the viewer pause for reflection to appreciate the beauty of nature and humanity that surrounds us every day.

24

Artist: Carla Maskall, www3.telus.net/maskall/carla.htm
Panel #24
Title: West Coast Spawning Salmon
Medium: Acrylic

wmunroe

by Wendy Munroe

Red Sky in the Morning

The native arbutus trees at the south end of our west coast island are sculpted by the prevailing south-easterly winter winds, as they take root and struggle for survival in the craggy red bluffs.

25

Artist: Wendy Munroe, http://www.pendercreatives.com/wendymunroe/index.html
Panel #25
Title: Red Sky in the Morning
Medium: Acrylic

Panel #026 by Christina Munck

untitled

26

Artist: Christina Munck, www.christinamunck.com
Panel #26
Title: untitled
Medium: Acrylic

Panel #027 by Nancy Ruhl

Tidal Pool Splash

One of the great things about coastal living is that the ocean is never far away. The warm and cool tones of this tile reminded me of low tide at Chesterman Beach on the West coast of Vancouver Island. I knew that I wanted to paint the sea and the beach and then introduce a figure enjoying both."

27

Artist: Nancy Ruhl, www.nancyruhl.com
Panel #27
Title: Tidal Pool Splash
Medium: Acrylic

L Pettit

Sticks Allison Shoreline

The beach access at Sticks Allison is one of our favourite spots for Plein Aire painting on Galiano Island.

28

Artist: Elisabeth Pettit,
Panel #28
Title: Sticks Allison Shoreline
Medium: Acrylic

Frog Clan

Shrouded in fog and mist for much of the year, totem poles of the West Coast Haida people stood along the coastal temperate rainforests, representing family lineages and privileges. The frog, seen here escaping from under the tail of a killer whale, is a symbol of that which is often misunderstood and underestimated, a possessor of wealth, and not to be insulted. If I had my choice I should choose to be a part of the frog clan because I have great admiration for these little creatures. This pacific tree frog, is a small (sometimes) brilliant green frog found throughout the southern part of the mainland and on Vancouver Island, as well as being introduced to Haida Gwaii.

29

Artist: Charity Dakin, www.charitydakin.com
Panel #29
Title: Frog Clan
Medium: Acrylic

Whale Dreams

30

Artist: Deb Garlick, www.debgarlick.com
Panel #30
Title: Whale Dreams
Medium: Acrylic

The Coastal Wolf

The wolf figures prominently in the folklore and beliefs of B.C.'s Coastal natives. It was once the central part of ceremonial life, with the Tlu-kwa-na or wolf ritual surpassing all others in importance. The wolf's shrewdness and predatory prowess was admired by all. This wolf is almost alive as it will follow you around.

31

Artist: John Stone, www.johnstonepaintings.com
Panel #31
Title: The Coastal Wolf
Medium: Acrylic

shot Nasser

Panel #032 by Sher Nasser

July Sunset

The inspiration for my panel painting is the result of the memories of the long sunset walks my siblings and I would take on Beach Avenue near English Bay Park. For a number of years we all visited Vancouver towards the end of July each year, to visit mom who lived on Davie Street. At the beach we would often stop to admire the rock figurine "Inukshuks" resting in the July sunset, put together by some beach loving artistic people. They always gave me a sense of inner peace.

32

Artist: Sher Nasser, www.shernasser.com
Panel #32
Title: July Sunset
Medium: Acrylic

Heron

For the bird, I used as source material, photographs I took of some herons at Pitt Lake (East of Vancouver).   The grassy shores were composed from photos of Burnaby Lake and Deer Lake in Burnaby BC.

33

Artist: Wolf Schenke, www.wolfschenke.com
Panel #33
Title: Heron
Medium: Acrylic

Panel #034   by Geneviève Gillett

Wonders of the West Coast

$$34$$

Artist: Geneviève Gillett, http://nsartists.ca/genevievegillett
Panel #34
Title: Wonders of the West Coast
Medium: Acrylic

Panel #035 by Marcia DeVique

Harvest Moon

35

Artist: Marcia DeVique
Panel #35
Title: Harvest Moon
Medium: Fused/Painted Glass

BERNADETTE '09

Panel #036   by Bernadette McCormack

When The Tide Recedes

36

Artist: Bernadette McCormack, www.bernadettemccormack.com
Panel #36
Title: When The Tide Recedes
Medium: Acrylic

Circle of Life

This project was a wonderful experience and at the time there was talk about the extinction of the salmon. I wanted to paint the circle of the salmon's life cycle in the laying of eggs and swimming the Pacific and I also represented the predetors they deal with in that cycle. On the top was a representation of the Spirit of that life in a serpent. I feel if given another chance to participate I could do something more inspirational.

37

Artist: Simon Daniel James, www.raventales.com
Panel #37
Title: Circle of Life
Medium: Acrylic

Willows' Beach

I once heard a scientist explain the effect of the Rayleigh Scattering.
Atmospheric particles, the same size of the wavelengths of visible light
cause the white light to split resulting in a sky-blue noon.
And that a red sunrise is the result of the short blue violet rays
scattering as sunlight passes diagonally through the atmosphere
leaving the longer waves of reds, oranges and yellow to be
received by the observing eye.
I wonder though, as I walk Willows Beach Esplanade,
if instead of the scientific reasoning of, wave lengths,
atmospheric particles, and distance from the sun,
that really it is Mother at play, with a flicker of her red flamboyance
rewarding me for not rolling over when the six am alarm bell rings.

38

Artist: Ingrid Fawcett, www3.telus.net/ingridfawcett
Panel #38
Title: Willows' Beach
Medium: Acrylic

Panel #039   by Barbara Parkin

My West Light

39

Artist: Barbara Parkin, www.barbaraparkin.com
Panel #39
Title: My West Light
Medium: Acrylic

Panel #040   by Teresa Gaye Hitch

Under the Westcoast Sky

I chose this tile because it reminded me of the view from my Westcoast home on Mt. Belcher (Salt Spring Island), overlooking the Pacific Ocean, the Gulf Islands (Galiano Island), and the Coastal Mountain range. "Under the Westcoast Sky" is the first painting I have created since my painting hand was seriously injured a few months ago. The honour of being invited to participate in Kunamokst,   a culturally and historically significant collaborative work of art, inspired me to overcome the challenges presented by the injury. Thank you, Kunamokst, for breaking the injury's hold on my painting practices!

40

Artist: Teresa Gaye Hitch, www.teresagayehitch.com
Panel #40
Title: Under the Westcoast Sky
Medium: Acrylic

The Run

The words "West Coast" and "salmon" go hand in hand. Salmon have been an integral feature in the survival of First Nations people and they continue to be part of an important food and fishing industry for BC. Unfortunately over-fishing, pollution, and land developments have endangered this most important species and the salmon runs have decreased in numbers over the years. I painted this panel to recognize the importance of this wild species of fish to our culture, our way of life.

41

Artist: Louise Nicholson, http://nsartists.ca/louisenicholson/
Panel #41
Title: The Run
Medium: Acrylic

Coucher De Soleil

Dans un ciel embrasé de ses propres feux, le soleil va bientôt disparaître dans les profondeurs du Pacifique, faisant place au voile de la nuit qui enveloppera la Côte jusqu'à l'aube... SUNSET. In a sky ablaze with its own fire, the sun is about to sink into the depths of the Pacific beckoning to the shadows of night to embrace the Coast until dawn..

42

Artist: Paulyne Deschamps-Peltier,
Panel #42
Title: Coucher De Soleil
Medium: Acrylic

GORDON HENSHELL

November Morning – Mid-Coast

This painting is in Mackenzie Sound, one of the inlets leading off Queen Charlotte Strait. There are nearly 300 Resident Orcas in the area each summer, following the salmon runs. This is November when there are just a few remaining Orcas searching for the Chum or "Dog" salmon that run this time of year. November rains have usually appeared and the area is filled with clouds and mist.

43

Artist: Gordon Henschel, www.henschelfinearts.com
Panel #43
Title: November Morning – Mid-Coast
Medium: Acrylic

Underwater Sunshine

I love the way the suns light reflects into water and creates amazing playgrounds for our underwater creatures.

Artist: Kelly Everill, www.kellysart.ca
Panel #44
Title: Underwater Sunshine
Medium: Acrylic

ALERT BAY
B.C.
-CIRCA 1890-

by Beth Dunlop

Alert Bay BC - circa 1890

Located on the northern Gulf Islands of BC, Alert Bay is a beautiful thriving community with a rich cultural history that exists on into today.

45

Artist: Beth Dunlop, www.bethdunlop.com
Panel #45
Title: Alert Bay BC - circa 1890
Medium: Acrylic

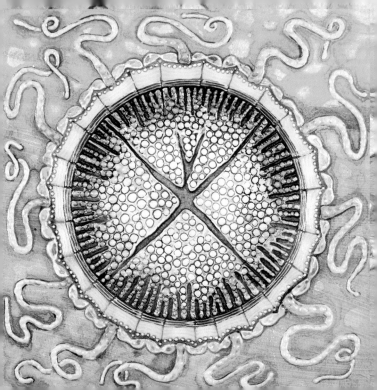

Glow with the Flow

The ocean is full of creatures that are so beautiful. Perhaps it is the water that enhances their beauty, making them look so graceful as they float along, or flutter their tentacles & translucent membranes. One of my favourite creatures is the Sea Anemone. It is like an ocean flower, round in shape and tentacles for petals. Some anemones are fluorescent and glow in the dark. Inspired by this, I have used fluorescent and glow paint which makes it come alive in the dark.

46

Artist: Heather Brewster, www.heatherbrewster.com
Panel #46
Title: Glow with the Flow
Medium: Acrylic, interference & glow paint

Panel #047   by Melodie Douglas

Seaside Treasures

47

Artist: Melodie Douglas, www.melodiedouglas.com
Panel #47
Title: Seaside Treasures
Medium: Acrylic

Moving On...

I was drawn to panel #48, then put some paint on it to find out why.

48

Artist: Vladimir Horik, www.vladimirhorik.com
Panel #48
Title: Moving On...
Medium: Oil

Looking West

There's just something mystical about watching the sun sink into the sea.

49

Artist: Tammy Woolgar, www.members.shaw.ca/woolgarstudio
Panel #49
Title: Looking West
Medium: Acrylic

Panel #050   by Steve Baylis

Catch of the Day

50

Artist: Steve Baylis, www.stevebaylis.com
Panel #50
Title: Catch of the Day
Medium: Oil

Tide Out

51

Artist: Lewis Lavoie www.lavoiestudios.com
Panel #51
Title: Tide out
Medium: Acrylic

Spirit of the Ocean

Whales, those ancient, magnificent, beings are believed to hold the secrets of the Universe...

They are gracious in their own way and only want us to respect and honour them and all living beings. May we be able to do so someday... starting with respecting and honouring ourselves and the sacredness of who we are!

52

Artist: Christine Poulin, www.christinepoulin.com
Panel #52
Title: Spirit of the Ocean
Medium: Acrylic

Undulating Flotsam

No westcoast mural is complete without showing the undulating ocean and driftwood

53

Artist: Karel Doruyter, www.studiokd.ca
Panel #53
Title: Undulating Flotsam
Medium: Acrylic

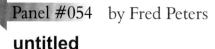

Panel #054   by Fred Peters

untitled

54

Artist: Fred Peters, www.fredpetersfineart.com
Panel #54
Title: untitled
Medium: Acrylic

Panel #055   by Rachel Daws

?work in progress?

On the west coast : A million tides, sculpt soft sandstone into petrified echos of it's own constant movement.

The ocean garden grows seaweed of many hues. Abundant are amber, brown and green but also purple and crimson. Amongst these are, Coral leaf, turkish wash cloth and sea lace, which when woven by waves and cast apon the beach, dry into amazing shades of red.

55

Artist: Rachel Daws, www.racheldaws.com
Panel #55
Title: ?work in progress?
Medium: Acrylic

Wasgo and the Spirit Hunters

The Sea Monster Wasgo is portrayed on the back of a barnacled Whale in the foreground, The Salmon spirits retreat underwater just above Wasgo. The canoeists in a traditional Haida boat represent the spirits of ancestors past. In the background the killer whales play and their departed ancestors follow behind them. Wherever we go we are one with those who came before us ~ a collective memory

56

Artist: Elissa Anthony, www.monelissastudio.com
Panel #56
Title: Wasgo and the Spirit Hunters
Medium: Acrylic

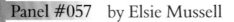

untitled

These playful creatures are often found among our coastal deciduous evergreens,- the arbutus- with its distinctive red bark.

57

Artist: Elsie Mussell
Panel #57
Title: untitled
Medium: Acrylic

Panel #058   by Darryl Albert

Sunset Paddle

Life on the coast of BC is truly wonderful. I like to spend time exploring with my kayak and gathering reference for my watercolour paintings. The sunsets are so inspiring and lately this is my favorite subject to paint.

58

Artist: Darryl Albert, www.darrylalbert.com
Panel #58
Title: Sunset Paddle
Medium: Watercolour

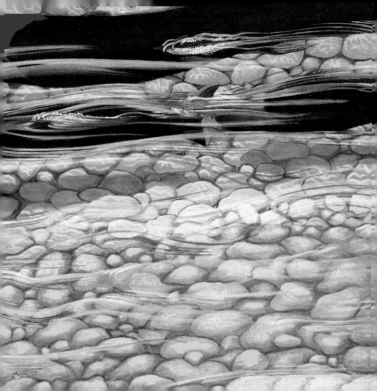

Panel #059   by Peter Lawson

Swim for Life

I've never forgotten the first time I stood in a river among hundreds of spawning salmon, swimming upstream past my legs. Their crimson colouring seemed appropriate to the spectacle of thrashing fish on their way to mate, deposit eggs and die shortly after...literally, a swim for life.

59

Artist: Peter Lawson, www.peterlawson.ca
Panel #59
Title: Swim for Life
Medium: Acrylic

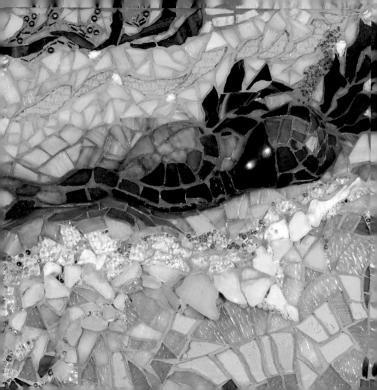

Bull Kelp Love

60

Artist: Deblekha Guin
Panel #60
Title: Bull Kelp Love
Medium: mosaic of beach glass, beads, shells, stained glass

Olivia

When I go to the beach, I go to think; to reconnect, to look at what is way bigger than my own "stuff" and get things back in perspective. It all started with being blessed with moments like this in my childhood - a nearby beach, where it didn't matter what I was building, but that I was able to lose myself in the sand and sea air and sound of waves.

61

Artist: Renay Piper, www.renaypiper.com
Panel #61
Title: Olivia
Medium: Acrylic

S. HARTFIEL

Panel #062   by Sharleen Hartfiel

West Coast Arbutus

The arbutus tree was the first thing I thought of when I was considering what to paint for this west coast mural project. Arbutus trees can often be found overlooking the ocean on Vancouver Island and the Gulf Islands in B.C.

62

Artist: Sharleen Hartfiel, www.sharleenhartfiel.com
Panel #62
Title: West Coast Arbutus
Medium: Acrylic

Panel #063   by Miranda Hebert

Western Waves

Living on the west coast brings me a sense of joy I can't explain. One of my favorite things to do is walk along the shore, listen to the waves, and feel the soft breeze coming from the ocean. I find it so peaceful and inspiring.

63

Artist: Miranda Hebert
Panel #63
Title: Western Waves
Medium: Acrylic

WYLAND ©2009

Panel #064   by Wyland

Sea Turtle Silhouette

64

Artist: Wyland, www.wyland.com
Panel #64
Title: Sea Turtle Silhouette
Medium: Acrylic

Surfacing in Stillness (Orca)

65

Artist: Christine "Keena" Friedrichsmeier   www.keena.ca
Panel #65
Title: Surfacing in Stillness (Orca)
Medium: Acrylic

Flight over the West Coast

Peaceful ocean with rocky shores, Vancouver surrounded by mountains rising among green trees, and flying Blue Herons - that is what I see when I think about the West Coast.

66

Artist: Iryna Nikitinska, www.uniquelyoursart.com
Panel #66
Title: Flight over the West Coast
Medium: Acrylic

Rolling In

As the waves come rolling in , little tidal pools form with sand bars in between. Eventually the tidal pools fill with water and the sand bars disappear .You will often see shore birds patrolling the beaches feeding on whatever is uncovered in the exposed sand.

67

Artist: Yvette Lantz, www.natureartists.com/yvette_lantz.asp
Panel #67
Title: Rolling In
Medium: oil

untitled

68

Artist: Ziggy Linklater, www.afishdaily.blogspot.com
Panel #68
Title: untitled
Medium: Acrylic

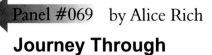 Panel #069   by Alice Rich

Journey Through

69

Artist: Alice Rich www.alice-rich.com
Panel #69
Title: Journey Through
Medium: Acrylic

Cold Poached Salmon

Guess what we're having for dinner?

70

Artist: Robert Nelmes   www.heavenlydeals.com
Panel #70
Title: Cold poached salmon
Medium: Acrylic

Panel #071 by Lewis Lavoie

Bait

71

Artist: Lewis Lavoie, www.lavoiestudios.com
Panel #71
Title: Bait
Medium: Acrylic

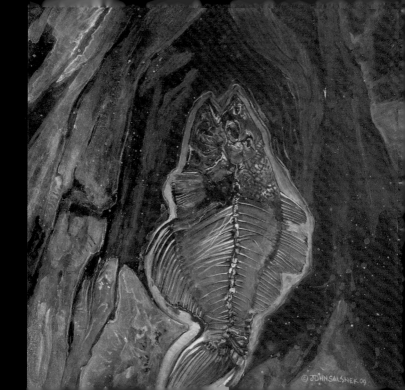
© JOHN SALSNEK 09

Panel #072   by John Salsnek

Stone Dead

This fossil fish is from the Eocene Period and found in North America

72

Artist: John Salsnek, www.artofjohnsalsnek.com
Panel #72
Title: Stone Dead
Medium: Acrylic

A "Day in the Life" of the Great Bear Rainforest

"We are so very proud how the act of painting is able to bring such grand focus and awareness toward preserving the 'Grizzly' Through issues concerning the endangerment of these great bears using this creative means is to capture the true spirit of these bears that is so beneficial toward saving life its self! Truly they are part of life's circle. Our inheritance and trust for all the generation now and to come"

73

Artist: Daniel Taylor, www.wildartafrica.org
Panel #73
Title: A "Day in the Life" of the Great Bear Rainforest
Medium: Acrylic

The Coastal Redwood Forest

The sheer size of the trees overwhelms you. Your fingers disappear into the crease of the bark. You look up, and become dizzy trying to establish where the tree ends and heaven begins.

74

Artist: Lewis Lavoie, www.lavoiestudios.com
Panel #74
Title: The Coastal Redwood Forest
Medium: Acrylic

Salal and Salmon

Being ecologically concerned, I was impressed when a visiting biologist explained that the leathery leaves of salal were designed to act as a protection for the top soil in the forest. When rain hits the leaves it rolls off gently and seeps to the forest floor. The relationship is somehwat symbiotic. And salmon- the staple food of the First Nations- both are definite coastal symbols. Currently salal is harvested and exported for use in bouquets. The leathery berries can be eaten.

75

Artist: Roxsane K Tiernan
Panel #75
Title: Salal and Salmon
Medium: Acrylic

Les Visiteurs Arrivèrent

This is a tribute to when various tribes from the west coast would come together wearing ceremonial masks.
A 'community' of paintings is forming a whale.
The whales, when they beach themselves on the shore, they are telling us that we are not respecting the ocean and consequently we are all in danger.
They bring the notion of planet as a community.

76

Artist: Raymond Martin, www.peterbucklandgallery.ca
Panel #76
Title: Les Visiteurs Arrivèrent
Medium: Acrylic

Spirit Mask

The mask and face combined together is depicting how many West Coast nations today are struggling to maintain their cultural identities.

77

Artist: Dennis J. Weber, www.webergallery.com
Panel #77
Title: Spirit Mask
Medium: Acrylic

Life On the Reef

78

Artist: Nancy McPhee
Panel #78
Title: Life On The Reef
Medium: Acrylic

Panel #079 by Brian Buckrell

Rocks and Reflections

Impressionistic view of typical west coast scene combining shoreline rocks with reflections of trees and sky

79

Artist: Brian Buckrell, www.brianbuckrell.com
Panel #79
Title: Rocks and Reflections
Medium: Acrylic

Panel #080   by Laura Kaardal

Tree

When I paint scenery, I tend to lean towards a simplified colour palette and reduce the shapes and lines in the image. What you see is what you get: sky, water, rocks, and tree.

80

Artist: Laura Kaardal, www.laurakaardal.com
Panel #80
Title: Tree
Medium: Acrylic

Panel #081   by Rob Elphinstone

Coast and Trees

My Actualism art is an attempt to capture the aspects of landscape that are seldom captured by Realism, other art movements or by photography. These are but a shadow of the reality that could be expressed.

81

Artist: Rob Elphinstone, www.members.shaw.ca/robelphinstone
Panel #81
Title: Coast and Trees
Medium: Oil

Free Spirit

Here in Kelowna, B.C., Christmas and winter bring us the beautiful trumpeter swans to visit where they can still swim and find food in the open water of Okanagan Lake. I feel so privileged to see them and have always wanted to paint them. I take countless photos while my fingers freeze in the cold wind. When the wind blows they ruffle their feathers, flap their wings and make their magical trumpeting sounds. It inspires me to know that they are also residents and visitors on the West Coast. I have only been able to pay short visits to the Coast and have not actually seen them there. I hope to do many more paintings of them in the future.

82

Artist: Theresa Eichler, www.natureartists.com/theresa_eichler.asp
Panel #82
Title: Free Spirit
Medium: Oil

The Guardian of the Heritage

The Killer Whales are part of numerous West Coast Tribal legends; they symbolize longevity and the guardian of the sea, strength and communication. The moon is known as the guardian of Mother Earth, protector of the people and is a symbol of power. It plays an important role in Northwest Native culture; various tribes believe that direction, vision and guidance could be received when it is bright. Totem poles are the legacy of the North West Tribes. This fabulous art form was made famous. What a beautiful idea to associate the moon, the guardian of the sea and in the same time give tribute to ancestral stories and art.

83

Artist: Patricia Gulyas, www.arpadcreation.com
Panel #83
Title: The guardian of the heritage
Medium: Acrylic

Humpback Harmony

When I first moved to British Columbia I heard about the whales that filled the west coast waters. Coming from Winnipeg, there were no mountains or ocean. Last summer as I flew back into Vancouver from my summer vacation in Manitoba, I was lucky enough to catch a glimpse of the silhouette of a Humpback whale below me. Humpback whales are known for their magical songs, which travel for great distances through the world's oceans. These sequences of moans, howls, cries, and other noises are quite complex and often continue for hours on end. It is most likely that humpbacks sing to communicate with others and to attract potential mates.

84

Artist: Ziggy Linklater, www.afishdaily.blogspot.com
Panel #84
Title: Humpback Harmony
Medium: Acrylic

Panel #085   by Marilyn Harris

Gulf Islands--Incoming Storm

85

Artist: Marilyn Harris, www.marilynharrisart.com
Panel #85
Title: Gulf Islands--Incoming Storm
Medium: Acrylic

Valerie Rogers

The Watcher

The edge of the sea is alive with possibilities.

86

Artist: Valerie Rogers, www.valerierogers.com
Panel #86
Title: The Watcher
Medium: Acrylic

Panel #087   by Janice Prevedoros

Surf

Over the next breaking wave,
Surfacing dark shapes curve.
Sunrise and sprays of mist,
Shaking loose like pearls.

Strands of submerged songs,
Ocean channels - echoing down the depths.

On aquatic ferris wheels, top fins wave like wild banners.
Slowly turning over, in their infinite watery ways.
Sprays of mist,
Shake loose like pearls.

87

Artist: Janice Prevedoros, www.janiceprevedoros.com
Panel #87
Title: Surf
Medium: Acrylic

Panel #088   by Lewis Lavoie

Lost in Sand Dollars

88

Artist: Lewis Lavoie, www.lavoiestudios.com
Panel #88
Title: Lost in Sand Dollars
Medium: Acrylic

Panel #089   by Kindrie Grove

Running the Gauntlet

89

Artist: Kindrie Grove, www.kindriegrove.com
Panel #89
Title: Running the Gauntlet
Medium: Acrylic

Humpback Whale

Humpback whales can easily be identified by their stocky bodies with obvious humps and black dorsal coloring. The head and lower jaw are covered with knobs called tubercles, which are actually hair follicles and are characteristic of the species.

90

Artist: Lewis Lavoie, www.lavoiestudios.com
Panel #90
Title: Humpback Whale
Medium: Acrylic

Panel #091   by Ian Sheldon

Storm at Sea

91

Artist: Ian Sheldon, www.iansheldon.com
Panel #91
Title: Storm at Sea
Medium: Oil

by Reb Benno

Orca-stral Suite

Living on Galiano island we have the occasional delight of seeing orcas traveling in pods and like at the peak of the crescendo one mighty orca breaches, leaping high into the air creating great excitement for all of us land-bound bipeds.

92

Artist: Reb Benno, www.muralguy.blogspot.com
Panel #92
Title: Orca-stral Suite
Medium: Acrylic

Raven

The raven has gravitas. This is perhaps because of intelligence as well as large size and serious black colour. There is nothing frivolous about the raven; even so, ravens enjoy playing, performing impressive aerobatics seemingly for the joy of it. Their vocalizations go beyond mere bird cries - they seem to almost talk to each other.

The raven has a privileged position in many native cultures as a trickster - he is the hero of disorder, transformation and change. In legend, it is the raven who found mankind in a clamshell, cracked it open and released us into the world.

93

Artist: Robert Bateman, www.robertbateman.ca
Panel #93
Title: Raven
Medium: Acrylic

Panel #094   by Lewis Lavoie

The Crew

The Canadian west coast has a thriving film industry. This panel is dedicated to Red Letter Films who created the documentary titled "The Eye of The Whale" which profiles the creation of this mural from start to finish.

94

Artist: Lewis Lavoie, www.lavoiestudios.com
Panel #94
Title: The Crew
Medium: Acrylic

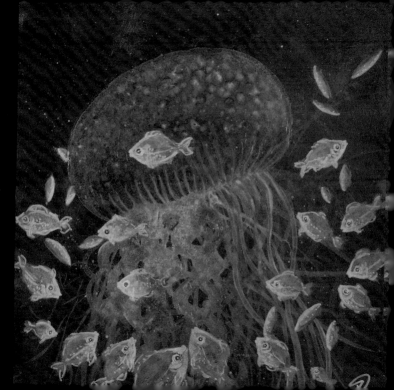

Jellyfish

The Lion's Mane Jellyfish (Cyanea capillata) is the largest known species of jellyfish. It is found in the cold waters of the Arctic, northern Atlantic and northern Pacific Oceans. In the open ocean, lion's mane jellyfish act as floating cities for certain species of fish providing food and protection from prey.

95

Artist: Vanessa Turke, www.vanessaturke.net
Panel #95
Title: Jellyfish
Medium: Acrylic

LRIEHL

Panel #096   by Lisa Riehl

Mussels & Anemone

This painting was inspired by the many trips I have taken to the beaches of Vancouver Island.   I've always been fascinated by the life that exists underwater – I actually have a B.Sc. degree in Zoology, where I took a ton of invertebrate zoology courses (and loved them!).   The many tidal pools in the nooks and crannies of the rocks during low tide are just a glimpse into this fascinating underwater world.   And since I was just recently in Tofino, I found a few great examples of mussels and sea anemones to paint.

96

Artist: Lisa Riehl, www.lisariehl.com
Panel #96
Title: Mussels & Anemone
Medium: Acrylic

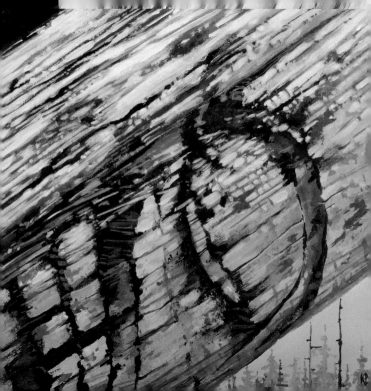

Panel #097 by Karel Doruyter

Past and Present

The first nation peoples are front and centre on the westcoast. I did a falling, deteriorating totem pole which I saw on Skedans, Haida Gwaii.

97

Artist: Karel Doruyter, www.studiokd.ca
Panel #97
Title: Past and Present
Medium: Acrylic

Three for the Show

After seeing sea lions through coin operated binoculars, we rented a 14 foot boat at Uculelet and headed for the open sea. We encountered 10, 20 and then 30 foot swells. We saw a ship at the top of the swell and not again for 10-15 minutes. Ready to turn back we spotted them. Frank focused on riding the swells. Thrilled, I shot two rolls. Suddenly the big bull dove into the water with a tremendous splash. The boat rental severely reprimanded us for going outside the protected cove and told that the plane overhead had been the Coast Guard! No harm done except I think I my have cracked the seat from repeatedly hitting it with my butt.

98

Artist: Helena Ball, www.helenaball.com
Panel #98
Title: Three for the Show
Medium: Acrylic

Siwash Rock

Siwash Rock is a famous rock outcropping found on the northwest side of Stanley Park in Vancouver, B. C. A legend among the indigenous Squamish Nation surrounds the origin of the rock. It guards the entrance to Burrard Inlet and Vancouver Harbour. The view in the painting is from the seawall looking north toward West Vancouver.

A plaque near the rock states that it is "Skalsh the unselfish" transformed by "Q'uas" as a reward for unselfishness.

99

Artist: Norman Vipond, http://nsartists.ca/normvipond
Panel #99
Title: Siwash Rock
Medium: Oil

Panel #100   by Chili Thom

The Power of Purple

100

Artist: Chili Thom, www.chilithom.com
Panel #100
Title: The Power of Purple
Medium: Acrylic

Panel #101   by Wendy Munroe

West Coast Sea Stacks

This kind of geological formation is found, not in the Gulf Islands where I live, but is typical of the west coast of Vancouver Island. Softer sedimentary rock has eroded away from steep-sided granite islets to reveal these "sea stacks". Thick fog banks roll in from the Pacific Ocean creating a soft and receding aerial perspective with suggestions of blue and violet. The panel presented to me included tones and shapes that brought to mind these soulful sea stacks.

101

Artist: Wendy Munroe, www.pendercreatives.com/wendymunroe/index.html
Panel #101
Title: West Coast Sea Stacks
Medium: Acrylic

S.S. BEAVER
1835   1882

SS Beaver

I have always been drawn to historical and charismatic architecture in my artwork. This painting features the SS Beaver, a replica of an earlier vessel that played an important role in British Columbia's coastal history. The SS Beaver was used for trading with the Hudson's Bay Company and also helped chart over 1500 km of B.C.'s coastline under Capt. Daniel Pender. It was rebuilt after its shipwreck in 1888, and after extensive refurbishing, it now hosts special functions and docks in Victoria, B.C.

102

Artist: Martin Machacek, www.martycultural.com
Panel #102
Title: SS Beaver
Medium: Acrylic

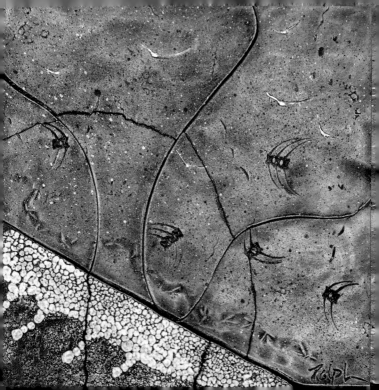

Panel #103   by Sandra Dolph

Swimming and Flying in the Sea

103

Artist: Sandra Dolph, www.sandradolph.com
Panel #103
Title: Swimming and Flying in the Sea
Medium: Ceramic Wall Reliefs

Diver

Living by the sea, I spend time on and in the water. I am aware of the sea as a source of life, and of our limitations in accessing its depths. As an artist, I am continually inspired by this source of life and the mysteries it contains.

104

Artist: Bruce Dolsen, www.brucedolsen.com
Panel #104
Title: Diver
Medium: Acrylic

by Tahirih Goffic

The Dancer

Since the focus of this mural project was the West Coast, I decided to focus on the culture of the aboriginal people of the Bella Coola valley in which I live, the Nuxalk. I was recently invited to the Children's Potlach, and was given permission by the chief to photograph the dances and to use them in my art, for which I feel greatly honored. Photographs of the Mask Dances in particular are not usually permitted. So I offer to you my interpretation of one, which I have simply titled, "The Dancer".

105

Artist: Tahirih Goffic, http://tahirihsblog.blogspot.com
Panel #105
Title: The Dancer
Medium: Acrylic

Panel #106   by Dorrie Ratzlaff

West Coast Under Attack by Fifty Foot Tall, Big Hair, Ultra-Thin Fashion Models

106

Artist: Dorrie Ratzlaff, www.dorrieratzlaff.com
Panel #106
Title: West Coast Under Attack by Fifty Foot Tall, Big Hair, Ultra-Thin Fashion Models
Medium: Acrylic

Daylight Surf

The painting shows the rolling sea with the daylight coming through the wave. You can almost hear the surf.

107

Artist: M. Shirley Thomas, www.shirleythomas.ca
Panel #107
Title: Daylight Surf
Medium: Oil

Blue Whale

The blue whale is a marine mammal belonging to the suborder of baleen whales . At up to 32.9 metres (108 ft) in length and 172 metric tons or more in weight, it is the largest animal ever known to have existed.

108

Artist: Lewis Lavoie, www.lavoiestudios.com
Panel #108
Title: Blue Whale
Medium: Acrylic

Panel #109   by Lewis Lavoie

Waiting for the Ferry

While relaxing on the comforts of the beautiful shore line on Galiano Island, one can wait peacefully and watch the ferry slowly pull into dock.

109

Artist: Lewis Lavoie, www.lavoiestudios.com
Panel #109
Title: Waiting for the ferry
Medium: Acrylic

Picking up Pebbles

The rocky beaches of British Columbia were some of my favorite family vacations as a child. Picking up rocks and seashells are a fond memory and I still enjoy walking down the beach with my eyes on the ground, searching for earth's little gems.

110

Artist: Denise Lefebvre, www.deniselefebvre.com
Panel #110
Title: Picking up Pebbles
Medium: Acrylic

Man Made Reefs

Historic or modern shipwrecks become unintended artificial reefs when preserved on the sea floor. Regardless of construction method, artificial reefs are generally designed to provide hard surfaces to which algae and invertebrates such as barnacles, corals, and oysters attach; the accumulation of attached marine life in turn provides intricate structure and food for assemblages of fish

111

Artist: Lewis Lavoie, www.lavoiestudios.com
Panel #111
Title: Man Made Reefs
Medium: Acrylic

The Black Bear

The Coastal Natives believed the black bear had the mystical powers to heal and protect them. Often the bear head is carved on their totem poles. Surprisingly, the black bear can come in many colors. One rare species of the black bear is the white Kermode or spirit bear. Most of them are found around Terrace, B.C.; although one was photographed in Juneau, Alaska. It is interesting that a black bear can have two cubs and one could be white and the other black or brown. Kermodes can also have black, white or shades of brown cubs.

112

Artist: John Stone, www.johnstonepaintings.com
Panel #112
Title: The Black Bear
Medium: Acrylic

April White
2009©

Tluu Jaad~Canoe Woman

The Haida Canoe's high bow cuts like a knife through the stormy turmoil of the open ocean. With hair and eagle feather tempest-swept, Tlúu Jaad's odyssey is to seek spiritual enlightenment. As Wind Spirit challenges her, the huntress sings a 'paddling song' while touching Flicker Feather's magic aura, thus summoning SGáan~Killerwhale. This Supernatural Being helps propel her into the spirit world, where all in the cosmos is there for knowing.

For the Haida, the reality of all worlds is through discovery in the cognitive process. An artist who conceives, then depicts these different dimensions, releases worlds beyond our consciousness.

113

Artist: April White, www.aprilwhite.com
Panel #113
Title: Tluu Jaad~Canoe Woman
Medium: Acrylic

Panel #114   by Pascal A. Pelletier

Blue Moon

What i wanted to share in this painting is the elder, looking west at the totem pole, at night , in the dark blue sky of the full moon , with the long house on the background. after i moved to the west coast, i have been welcome by a elder who introduce me to my culture and the art of the northwest coast carving, and the traditionnal ceremonies. paying tribute to the elder who carry the knowledges and wisdoms, carry the history. like totem poles, standing proud.

114

Artist: Pascal A.Pelletier, www.artmajeur.com/pascalapelletier
Panel #114
Title: Blue Moon
Medium: Acrylic and graphite

Blue Heron

I have lived on the west coast all my life where herons have always been in the background, from the shores of Galiano Island where they hunt alone, to the park down the street from my apartment in Vancouver's West End where hundreds of these gangly birds nest in the six trees that tower the noisy tennis courts. I have tried my best to represent one solitary heron here with machine appliqued fabric.

115

Artist: Cedar Bowers
Panel #115
Title: Blue Heron
Medium: old t-shirts, thread, and dye.

Panel #116 by Lewis Lavoie

Salmon Lifecycle

Atlantic salmon spend between one and four years at sea. Prior to spawning, depending on the species, salmon undergo changes. They may grow a hump, develop canine teeth and male salmon develop a pronounced curvature of the jaw called a kype. All will change from the silvery blue of a fresh run fish from the sea to a darker color.

116

Artist: Lewis Lavoie, www.lavoiestudios.com
Panel #116
Title: Salmon Lifecycle
Medium: Acrylic

Panel #117   by Lewis Lavoie

Someplace to Hide

117

Artist: Lewis Lavoie, www.lavoiestudios.com
Panel #117
Title: Someplace to Hide
Medium: Acrylic

Panel #118   by Lewis Lavoie

Tide

118

Artist: Lewis Lavoie, www.lavoiestudios.com
Panel #118
Title: Tide
Medium: Acrylic

VICTORIA ARMSTRONG

Breached

Orca's are the largest members of the dolphin family, and are found in all the world's oceans. Though not an international endangered species, local populations can be threatened or endangered due to loss of prey or habitat, pollution, capture by marine parks and conflict with fisheries. They are highly sophisticated social creatures, and there are many reasons attributed to their habit of "breaching". Like all members of the dolphin family, they have no difficulty in clearing the surface when they surge upward, and then hit the water with a satisfying "smack".

119

Artist: Victoria Armstrong, www.victoriaarmstrong.com
Panel #119
Title: Breached
Medium: Acrylic

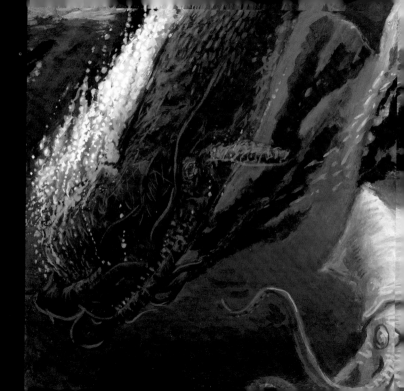

Panel #120   by Lewis Lavoie

Whale vs Squid

As two of the ocean's largest and most feared creatures, the sperm whale and the giant squid have fired the imaginations of storytellers for centuries.

120

Artist: Lewis Lavoie, www.lavoiestudios.com
Panel #120
Title: Whale vs Squid
Medium: Acrylic

Panel #121   by Ron Straight

Wings

Seagulls remind me of the wonderful freedom they must feel when flying, just like I felt when I left the prairies to come to the west coast... oh, so long ago. I find that painting gives me the same feeling!

The feather/wave represents the coastal water with the sparkle of the sun glinting. The green represents the coast forest greenery. The divide between the light and dark areas represents the coastline.

121

Artist: Ron Straight, http://rgstraight.shawwebspace.ca/
Panel #121
Title: Wings
Medium: Oil

Panel #122   by Tish Saunders

Looking North Up Georgia Strait from Galiano Island

Galiano Island is long and thin and in the middle a ridge of hills winds up the island like a spine. From the northeast side you look across to the Continent and up Georgia Strait. The sky is huge, the weather and light change constantly. A dark and rugged sky can hang over you while up ahead the ocean is brightening and the sky is clearing and light. The mountains can appear across the strait like a huge fortress and next minute, are covered in clouds with just the tops sticking through. I think its a beautiful place.

122

Artist: Tish Saunders, www.insightartgallery.ca
Panel #122
Title: Looking North up Georgia Strait from Galiano Island
Medium: Acrylic

Martha Ramirez

by Martha Ramirez

Whale Woman Regenerating Life

It was sad to see my whale woman go! I didn't realize how much she filled my space, my life. Her image of breathing healing movement into global troubled waters, electrified and inspired me into daily transformations. I know this collective effort of so many hearts, will contribute to balance and to regenerate "Tonantzin Tlalli" our Mother Earth!

123

Artist: Martha Ramirez
Panel #123
Title: Whale Woman Regenerating Life
Medium: Acrylic

Panel #124 by Brian Simons

Coastal Mountains

124

Artist: Brian Simons, www.briansimons.com
Panel #124
Title: Coastal Mountains
Medium: Acrylic

Wolf Eel

I decided on an underwater theme. I chose the wolf eel. Not a wolf nor an eel. It is an ugly fish that is friendly to scuba divers.I painted it somewhat diffused, practically drybrush. The eel is coming out of its lair to visit the sea cucumber or perhaps a diver.

125

Artist: Peter Moore, www.petermooreartist.com
Panel #125
Title: Wolf Eel
Medium: Acrylic

Panel #126   by Lea Price

Soaring Over the Peaks

To live in one of the most beautiful areas of the world invites visual sharing. We have the ocean, the rivers and the land, the mountains and the sky, the wild life, and marine life - all stimulating the creative juices to express wonderment in it all. Being able to see this from above like a soaring eagle, taking in the amazing freedom of flight, breathing in the pristine air, wings out, gliding over the forest of trees to the next vista was my inspiration for this panel.

126

Artist: Lea Price, www.leapriceartist.com
Panel #126
Title: Soaring Over the Peaks
Medium: Acrylic

Panel #127 by Bernadette McCormack

Porthole

127

Artist: Bernadette McCormack, www.bernadettemccormack.com
Panel #127
Title: Porthole
Medium: Acrylic

Panel #128   by Lewis Lavoie

Sun Beams and Seagulls

128

Artist: Lewis Lavoie, www.lavoiestudios.com
Panel #128
Title: Sun Beams and Seagulls
Medium: Acrylic

Panel #129   by Lewis Lavoie

Duty

To commemorate those in the service of The Canadian Pacific Railway Company who, at the call of King and country, left all that was dear to them, endured hardship, faced danger, and finally passed out of sight of men by the path of duty and self sacrifice, giving up their own lives that others might live in freedom. Let those who come after see to it that their names not be forgotten. Based on sculpture by Coeur de Lion McCarthy

129

Artist: Lewis Lavoie, www.lavoiestudios.com
Panel #129
Title: Duty
Medium: Acrylic

Panel #130   by Lewis Lavoie

Trail Mix

The superb terrain and the moderate climate make Vancouver Island, BC, a mecca for mountain biking. Active clubs and their members help maintain the numerous trails you will find throughout the island, ranging from easy family tracks to the very difficult rides that will challenge your physical fitness and your technical know-how

130

Artist: Lewis Lavoie, www.lavoiestudios.com
Panel #130
Title: Trail Mix
Medium: Acrylic

Sea Otter

The sea otter is one of the smallest marine mammal species. Unlike other marine mammals, the sea otter has no blubber and relies on its exceptionally thick fur to keep warm. With up to 150 thousand strands of hair per square centimeter (nearly one million per sq in), its fur is the most dense of any animal.

131

Artist: Lewis Lavoie, www.lavoiestudios.com
Panel #131
Title: Sea Otter
Medium: Acrylic

Panel #132 by Sylvia Leschyshyn

Haida Totems

Kunamokst. Haida totems bring together elements that are integral to the magnificence of the West Coast—sea, sky, rock, flora (particularly giant red cedar) and fauna, diverse culture and history, rich symbolism and artistry. Illustrated are totems of Haida Gwaii (Queen Charlotte Islands)—eagle—and Prince Rupert—portion of a pole bearing the striae of time.

132

Artist: Sylvia Leschyshyn
Panel #132
Title: Haida Totems
Medium: Acrylic

Panel #133   by Maria Buehl

Curious Seal

Harbor seals spend half their time on land and half in water. Harbor seals are curious mammals, and can be spotted watching humans walking on beaches or at docks. They are wary of people and if disturbed will rush away abandoning their favorite habitat spots and pups. "Curious Seal", reminded me of a harbor seal that would often watch me as I walked along the beach towards Tow Hill, on the Queen Charlotte Island

133

Artist: Maria Buehl, www.mariabuehl.com
Panel #133
Title: Curious Seal
Medium: Acrylic

Panel #134   by Phil Alain

Fishing In The Dark

The tranquil setting and mild evening weather on the west coast can allow for some precious moments of bonding.

134

Artist: Phil Alain, www.philalain.com
Panel #134
Title: Fishing In The Dark
Medium: Acrylic

K. Holmes

Moonlight on Hidden Beach, Active Pass, Galiano Island

Hidden Beach on Active Pass is part of Mathews Point Regional Park on Galiano Island. During the day marine traffic including ferries, seals, otters and orcas travel through the busy Pass. In the moonlight the sand and white shell beach fairly glow in the dark.

135

Artist: Keith Holmes, www.muralact.com
Panel #135
Title: Moonlight on Hidden Beach, Active Pass, Galiano Island
Medium: Acrylic

One Starry Night...

As two of the ocean's largest and most feared creatures, the sperm whale and the giant squid have fired the imaginations of storytellers for centuries.

136

Artist: Annette Shaw,   www.annetteshaw.ca
Panel #136
Title: One Starry Night...
Medium: Coloured pencil and gel pens on black paper

Panel #137 by Lewis Lavoie

Racing the Storm

Racing the Storm- Sailors must always keep an eye on the sky for as beautiful as the west coast scenery can be, Mother Nature can turn on you in a flash!

137

Artist: Lewis Lavoie, www.lavoiestudios.com
Panel #137
Title: Racing the Storm
Medium: Acrylic

Panel #138 by Lewis Lavoie

Fish Market

138

Artist: Lewis Lavoie, www.lavoiestudios.com
Panel #138
Title: Fish Market
Medium: Acrylic

Panel #139 by Lewis Lavoie

The Underwater Parade

139

Artist: Lewis Lavoie, www.lavoiestudios.com
Panel #139
Title: The Underwater Parade
Medium: Acrylic

Panel #140   by Michelle Grant

Still Waters

The elegance of the gull belies its aggressively opportunistic nature. Even though they are a common sight along the West Coast, I have always been drawn to their beautiful streamline form and subtle colouration.

140

Artist: Michelle Grant, www.michellegrant.ca
Panel #140
Title: Still Waters
Medium: Acrylic

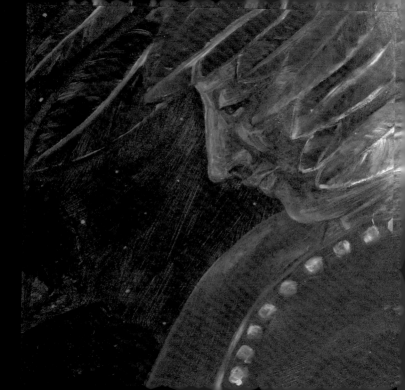

Panel #141   by Sarah Haxby

Raven Wind-Talker

This dream-like imagery was inspired by stories told to me by a West Coast traditional storyteller.

141

Artist: Sarah Haxby, www.peargirl.com
Panel #141
Title: Raven Wind-Talker
Medium: Acrylic

Panel #142   by Lewis Lavoie

Gold Rush

Victoria and its harbours became a hub of activity during the Alaskan Gold Rush.

142

Artist: Lewis Lavoie, www.lavoiestudios.com
Panel #142
Title: Gold Rush
Medium: Acrylic

James Koll

Panel #143   by James Koll

Portlock Point Lighthouse

Portlock Point Lighthouse is on Prevost Island, a lesser known Gulf Island nestled at the southern tip of Galiano. Built in 1896 and still in use today, it is visible from the ferry between Tswwassen and Swartz Bay. This painting is stylized from photos I took while departing from Pender Island by seaplane

143

Artist: James Koll, www.jameskoll.com
Panel #143
Title: Portlock Point Lighthouse
Medium: Acrylic

Panel #144   by Greg Cope

untitled

1 44

Artist: Greg Cope, www.shoreleave.com
Panel #144
Title: untitled
Medium: Acrylic

Orca and Calf

Orcas off Vancouver Island are a big deal here - wonderful and controversial.

145

Artist: Ron Wilson, www.artistwilson.com
Panel #145
Title: Orca and Calf
Medium: Acrylic

Galiano Island Sandstone

146

Artist: Larry Foden
Panel #146
Title: Galiano Island Sandstone
Medium: Acrylic

ShariErickson

Surf's Up

The Harlequin is one of my favourite duck species. They can be seen in surf right up alongside rocky headlands and jetties, diving deep underwater to feed. They nest in coastal mountain streams, often very secretive and hard to find. My panel came with a design that suggested rocks and surf, a perfect setting for this beautiful drake.

147

Artist: Shari Erickson, www.sharierickson.com
Panel #147
Title: Surf's Up
Medium: Acrylic

Panel #148 by Penny Prior

Bellbuoy

148

Artist: Penny Prior, www.pennyprior.com
Panel #148
Title: Bellbuoy
Medium: Acrylic

Panel #149 by Lewis Lavoie

Evening Crossing

149

Artist: Lewis Lavoie, www.lavoiestudios.com
Panel #149
Title: Evening Crossing
Medium: Acrylic

Panel #150 by Lewis Lavoie

Swim West

150

Artist: Lewis Lavoie, www.lavoiestudios.com
Panel #150
Title: Swim West
Medium: Acrylic

Coastal Awakening

151

Artist: Lewis Lavoie, www.lavoiestudios.com
Panel #151
Title: Coastal Awakening
Medium: Acrylic

Panel #152   by Lewis Lavoie

HMS Discovery 1776-79

Captain Cook commanded the ship the HMS Discovery northeast to explore the west coast of North America, landing near the First Nations village at Yuquot in Nootka Sound on Vancouver Island.

152

Artist: Lewis Lavoie, www.lavoiestudios.com
Panel #152
Title: HMS Discovery 1776-79
Medium: Acrylic

Panel #153 by Lewis Lavoie

The Watcher

153

Artist: Lewis Lavoie, www.lavoiestudios.com
Panel #153
Title: The Watcher
Medium: Acrylic

Panel #154   by Francine Renaud

The Sea Trouts

The gem like quality of a fish freshly out of water has kept me fascinated ever since I can remember. There is something so intriguing about Neptune's Kingdom. I enjoyed capturing through layers of glazes, the glistening of their bodies in a fluid environment. Their speckled backs and silvery colors are so very attractive to me. Of course their speckles are part of a very successful camouflage, a way of being invisible at a most vulnerable time. They spawn like salmon, on a gravel bed in the shallow waters of a riverbed.

154

Artist: Francine Renaud, www.francinerenaud.ca
Panel #154
Title: The Sea Trouts
Medium: Acrylic

The Blues

Blue mussels and barnacles - humble and ubiquitous - are essential parts of the infinitely complex web that supports all life in the cool waters of the Pacific NW.

155

Artist: Cindy Davis
Panel #155
Title: The Blues
Medium: Acrylic

Panel #156 by Rohana Laing

West Coast Boat Marina

This was a challenge to paint a painting that "worked" within the guidlines of a set compositon, values and colour tones.

156

Artist: Rohana Laing, www.rohanart.com
Panel #156
Title: West Coast Boat Marina
Medium: Acrylic

Mike Cerencser '09

Panel #157 by Mike Gerencser

The Migration

157

Artist: Mike Gerencser
Panel #157
Title: The Migration
Medium: Acrylic

KHolmes

Bear in Blue

It's strange that despite living 10 minutes from downtown Vancouver, I feel that being "bear aware" is still important. Living on the west coast means that in minutes I can be hiking or biking where bears are not an uncommon sight on the trails and roadways. I have been fortunate to have seen these beautiful creatures from a safe distance on several occasions during trips up and down the west coast of B.C. I am always intrigued how they have a certain gentle, lumbering way of moving along, when I know that they are also so powerful and agile.

158

Artist: Kathy Holmes, www.kathyandflick.com
Panel #158
Title: Bear in Blue
Medium: Acrylic

Panel #159   by Lewis Lavoie

The Swimmer

159

Artist: Lewis Lavoie, www.lavoiestudios.com
Panel #159
Title: The Swimmer
Medium: Acrylic

Panel #160   by Lewis Lavoie

Fallen Legends

When walking along the west coast one would imagine finding ancient artifacts

160

Artist: Lewis Lavoie, www.lavoiestudios.com
Panel #160
Title: Fallen Legends
Medium: Acrylic

Panel #161 by Lewis Lavoie

Carved Fish

161

Artist: Lewis Lavoie, www.lavoiestudios.com
Panel #161
Title: Carved Fish
Medium: Acrylic

Panel #162   by Lewis Lavoie

Atrevida Dining

The picturesque view one can enjoy while dining on Galiano Island

162

Artist: Lewis Lavoie, www.lavoiestudios.com
Panel #162
Title: Atrevida Dining
Medium: Acrylic

Porpoise Feast

163

Artist: Lewis Lavoie, www.lavoiestudios.com
Panel #163
Title: Porpoise Feast
Medium: Acrylic

Panel #164   by Maxine Wolodko

Autumn at Locarno Beach

This is a view I enjoy from near my home and is one of the best things about living in Vancouver.

164

Artist: Maxine Wolodko, www.wolodko.ca
Panel #164
Title: Autumn at Locarno Beach
Medium: Acrylic

Panel #165 by Virginia Chin

Undersea Garden

This painting represents my impressions of nature's precious sealife beneath the coastal waters, a wonderful world of colours, shapes and forms.

165

Artist: Virginia Chin, www3.telus.net/vicibi/Ginny%20Site/Welcome.html
Panel #165
Title: Undersea Garden
Medium: Acrylic

Panel #166   by Kirsten Carlson

Subtidal Passage

These are familiar friends, anytime I go diving on the West Coast. I sometimes glimpse Harbor seals cruising past my bubbles, but most often I see them napping just above the waves on near shore rocks. Although Painted Greenlings blend in unbelievably well with their surroundings, I can spy them amongst the swaying red algae. The fish eating anemones appear like ghostly white flowers in the underwater landscape. They have an interrelationship with Painted Greenlings just like some anemones in tropical seas have with clownfish. I am grateful for each dive-adventure I take because each time I see something new and wonderful in the underwater realm of the sea.

166

Artist: Kirsten Carlson, www.kirstencarlson.net
Panel #166
Title: Subtidal Passage
Medium: Acrylic

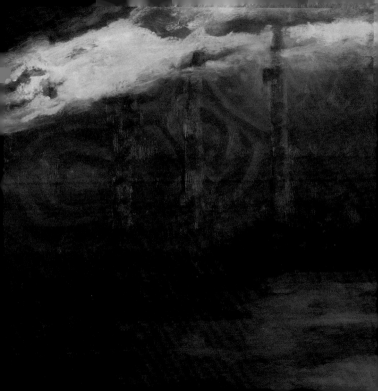

Bear Spirit

The Bear Spirit is represented in the background, being the whale the spectator. I tried to unify as much elements as possible that represent the West Coast: The sea, the Totem Poles, Great sunsets and the Bears.

167

Artist: Patricia Guzmán, http://patriciaguzman.blogspot.com/
Panel #167
Title: Bear Spirit
Medium: Oil

Artists of Antiquity

Petroglyphs have been found up and down the west coast, some dating back thousands of years. Present native populations have no knowledge about who created them or why and scholars can only speculate on their meaning. I know the artists who created them did so because they 'had' to. Creating art feeds the soul. So I wonder; were there deadlines to meet, was everyone a critic and when the last chip was excised from the granite boulder, did the artist sit back with a glass of wine and enjoy that wondrous feeling of accomplishment?

168

Artist: Barbara Would Schaefer
Panel #168
Title: Artists of Antiquity
Medium: Acrylic

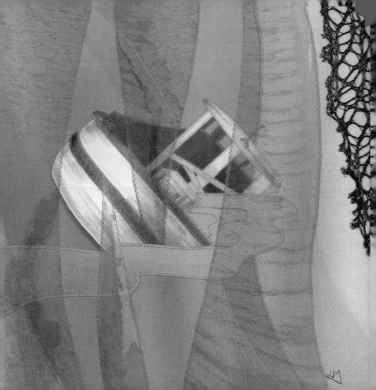

by Lea Elizabeth Mabberley

Coastal Sands

This fabric square is based on the image of a boat stranded below Rose Point, Queen Charlotte islands: and in memory of the many boats that have gone down to the sands off this coast.

169

Artist: Lea Elizabeth Mabberley
Panel #169
Title: Coastal Sands
Medium: Acrylic

Panel #170   by Lewis Lavoie

Tribute to Bill Reid

Raven Releasing the First People from a Huge Clam Shell- A tribute to Bill Reid's wood carving.

170

Artist: Lewis Lavoie, www.lavoiestudios.com
Panel #170
Title: Tribute to Bill Reid
Medium: Acrylic

Panel #171   by Lewis Lavoie

Underwater Magic

171

Artist: Lewis Lavoie, www.lavoiestudios.com
Panel #171
Title: Underwater Magic
Medium: Acrylic

Panel #172   by A.J Bell

Off Francis Peninsula

172

Artist: A.J Bell, www.ajbell.ca
Panel #160
Title: Off Francis Peninsula
Medium: Acrylic

Panel #173   by Wendy Palmer

Tofino Morning Fog

My family's favorite summer get away is Tofino on the west coast of Vancouver Island. The Wickaninnish Inn is the only resort on beautiful Chesterman Beach, which is where we enjoy many relaxing days watching waves and walking the beach. The driftwood is found all along the beach. The ocean possesses so many unknown adventures, and the foggy mornings on Chesterman Beach create a mysterious atmosphere of what the ocean has in store for us. As the fog breaks, the sun will hopefully emerge for another summer day, and we can enjoy surfing, sea kayaking or hiking around the island grasping its beauty and splendour.

173

Artist: Wendy Palmer, www.wendypalmer-artist.com
Panel #173
Title: Tofino Morning Fog
Medium: Acrylic

QUEEN OF CUMBERLAND

Panel #174   by Lewis Lavoie

Queen of Cumberland

174

Artist: Lewis Lavoie, www.lavoiestudios.com
Panel #174
Title: Queen of Cumberland
Medium: Acrylic

Captain Vancouver

Captain Vancouver was the mid shipman on Captain James Cook's 2nd voyage on the HMS Resolution. His charts of the North American northwest coast were so extremely accurate that they served as the key reference for coastal navigation for generations.

175

Artist: Lewis Lavoie, www.lavoiestudios.com
Panel #175
Title: Captain Vancouver
Medium: Acrylic

Panel #176 by Lewis Lavoie

Purple Starfish

176

Artist: Lewis Lavoie, www.lavoiestudios.com
Panel #176
Title: Purple Starfish
Medium: Acrylic

Coulthard

Swoosh

177

Artist: Eleanor Coulthard,   www.galiander.ca/Paintings
Panel #177
Title: Swoosh
Medium: Acrylic

by Catherine Marchand

Mermaid of B.C.

In 1967 off the West Coast of British Columbia, there was an actual sighting of a mermaid by passengers on B.C. Ferries. They saw her sitting on some rocks in Active Pass near Victoria. The Times Colonist newspaper at the time said "the mermaid had long blonde hair, the body of a porpoise from the waist down and was apparently eating a salmon when sighted." Who knows? Maybe she will pop up again, even if it's in my own imagination.

178

Artist: Catherine Marchand, www.4hisglorycreations.com
Panel #178
Title: Mermaid of B.C.
Medium: Acrylic

Ocean's Edge

Tidal pools are full of sunlight, sparkling color and wee creatures. My piece depicts these fascinating microcosms as they sit in proximity to the deeper, darker ocean.

179

Artist: Jackie Tahara, www.jackietahara.com
Panel #179
Title: Ocean's Edge
Medium: India ink, acrylic gouache, cut paper collage

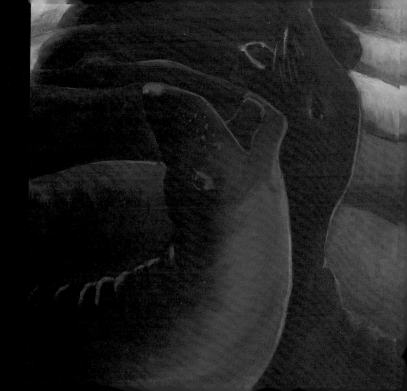

Howl at the Moon

180

Artist: Phil Alain, www.philalain.com
Panel #180
Title: Howl at the Moon
Medium: Acrylic

Panel #181   by Dianna Ponting

Button Blanket

West Coast ceremonial button blankets represent a 160-year-old aboriginal tradition that was influenced by goods introduced by 19th century traders. The blankets were originally acquired from the Hudson's Bay Company and decorated with buttons made from abalone or dentalium shells with a central crest typically portraying a symbol of the wearer's family heritage. They are still made and worn today at potlatches, ceremonial dances, weddings and graduations.

181

Artist: Dianna Ponting, www.ponting.com
Panel #181
Title: Button Blanket
Medium: Acrylic

Stawamus Chief Sun Climb

An internationally renowned destination by the world's climbing elite, the"Chief" was once deemed un- climbable. The Stawamus Chief remains an awe-inspiring monolith of granite and a sacred cultural and heritage site for the Squamish first nations. With slow carefully planned moves, the sun climber perseveres with dedication and respect for this incredible monument of nature...

The climber connects to his inner spirit, is charged by the sun and communes with the creator, as one.

182

Artist: Steven Miko Burns
Panel #182
Title: Stawamus Chief Sun Climb
Medium: Acrylic

Treasure Hunting

Even in Montreal I was fascinated by the west coast, especially the mountains and all the different beaches so close to the cities. So, with my boys, our favorite trips are ones where they can go treasure hunting for wild life and where my boys can be braver than their mom and touch every living thing! For me these precious moments make the west coast very special.

183

Artist: Sophie St-Pierre, www.uniquelyoursart.com
Panel #183
Title: Treasure Hunting
Medium: Acrylic

Panel #184   by Robert Ives

untitled

184

Artist: Robert Ives, www.ivesart.blogspot.com
Panel #184
Title: untitled
Medium: Acrylic

Michelle Goldsmith

California Sea Lions

If you have ever visited San Francisco's Pier 39, no doubt you either saw or heard the California Sea Lions which have taken up residence on the docks. They have become quite a tourist attraction with hundreds of them swimming or laying on the docks and often barking loudly. They also like to steal fish from commercial fishing boats. Because of this, some consider them to be a nuisance. At the turn of the 20th century, their numbers started rapidly decreasing, but thanks to the Marine Mammal Protection Act of 1972, their numbers stabilized and have since been steadily increasing.

185

Artist: Michelle Goll Smith, www.sketchycharacters.com
Panel #185
Title: California Sea Lions
Medium: Acrylic

Reflections of Red

My landscape paintings are stylized and boldly coloured images of the west coast with its many islands, rocky shores and majestic trees that cling to its coast line.

186

Artist: Jeanette Jarville, www.jeanettejarville.com
Panel #186
Title: Reflections of Red
Medium: Acrylic

Panel #187   by Stephanie Gauvin

Exploring the Coast

187

Artist: Stephanie Gauvin, www.artiststephaniegauvin.com
Panel #187
Title: Exploring the Coast
Medium: Acrylic

Treasures of the Sea

Having never snorkelled until a couple of years ago, I was amazed and excited about all the colours and life abounding under the water, that until then I had been completely unaware of. It was a beautiful discovery that has me hooked now to see any chance I get!

188

Artist: Ramona Swift, www.swiftfox.ca
Panel #188
Title: Treasures of the Sea
Medium: Acrylic

Northwest Arthropods

*I chose the prolific crabs that populate the Puget Sound as the subject for
my panel. When I finished the panel I was reminded of the tiny
creatures I once saw through my brother's powerful microscope while
visiting him at King's College in Edmonton. He had collected the speck
of dirt locally and had his students looking at soil organisms and
identifying what they saw.*

*Turns out those microscopic crablike creatures are called Oribatidae and
are actually arthropods like crabs. Oribatidae are very common in our
soils, especially on the West Coast.*

189

Artist: Geri Peterson, www.geripeterson.com
Panel #189
Title: Northwest Arthropods
Medium: Acrylic

M. Conley

The Raven

I was thrilled to participate in this artistic adventure. The raven was a logical choice for me. This magnificent bird inhabits the Pacific Northwest and is revered in indigenous mythology.

190

Artist: Mary Conley, www.artworksbymaryconley.com
Panel #190
Title: The Raven
Medium: Acrylic

Panel #191   by Lewis Lavoie

Emily Carr's Forest

A tribute to Emily Carr

191

Artist: Lewis Lavoie, www.lavoiestudios.com
Panel #191
Title: Emily Carr's Forest
Medium: Acrylic

Northwesterly

Northwesterly began it's life as, "Mother Ocean". One day I stood and looked at the sea and realized it is part of the sky. I stood beside Ksien, "the juice from the clouds", the Skeena River, and realized the moisture comes from the sky and returns to the land and eventually flows to the sea only to return to the sky once again. We say the sky is our father and the earth is our mother and we are all the children. So what I've always called Mother Ocean because someone taught me that is really our father as it is one with the sky. So I came to rename this piece, The Northwesterly. The northwest wind is a good one, it keeps the skies clear. There are some who fear the winds that blow; I'm not one of those. I find pleasure in the wind; I hear the songs of our ancestors on the air.

192

Artist: Roy Henry Vickers, www.royhenryvickers.com
Panel #192
Title: Northwesterly
Medium: Acrylic

Rhythm of the Waves

The ever changing west coast waves rushing to the rocky beach creating the rhythm of the waves.

193

Artist: Howard Ku, www.howardku.com
Panel #193
Title: Rhythm of the Waves
Medium: Oil

Safe Harbour

As an artist, being Dutch and living in Canada is almost symbolic of a "safe harbour"; the Canadian liberation of The Netherlands of 1945 is not forgotten. If it were not for them, I wouldn't have been born!

194

Artist: Jeanne Krabbendam, www.jeannekrabbendam.com
Panel #194
Title: Safe Harbour
Medium: acrylics/ graphite / water colour pencil / mixed media

Panel #195 by Lewis Lavoie

Moonlight

195

Artist: Lewis Lavoie, www.lavoiestudios.com
Panel #195
Title: Moonlight
Medium: Acrylic

Panel #196 by Lewis Lavoie

The Perch

196

Artist: Lewis Lavoie, www.lavoiestudios.com
Panel #196
Title: The Perch
Medium: Acrylic

Deep Woods

"Deep Woods" was inspired by walking in the woods, looking down at my feet and observing many small creatures who live and hunt amongst the pine cones and leaf mould.

197

Artist: Diane Laronde
Panel #197
Title: Deep Woods
Medium: Acrylic

Banister

Dolphins Dance

198

Artist: Cyndee Banister
Panel #198
Title: Dolphins Dance
Medium: Oil

Panel #199   by Gary Whitley

From Twilight to New Dawn

Over a century ago the impact of European culture suffocated many indigenous cultures and their art. This painting is an attempt to show that impact by the totems in a night scene. The other totem is painted in colors suggesting the current on going emergence of the indigenous west coast art scene. An art genre far too sophisticated and precious to be ignored.

199

Artist: Gary Whitley
Panel #199
Title: From Twilight to New Dawn
Medium: Oil

On The Rocks

Rocks below the tideline of the ocean shore provide a smorgasbord for gulls.

200

Artist: Marion Rose, www.marionrose.com
Panel #200
Title: On The Rocks
Medium: Acrylic

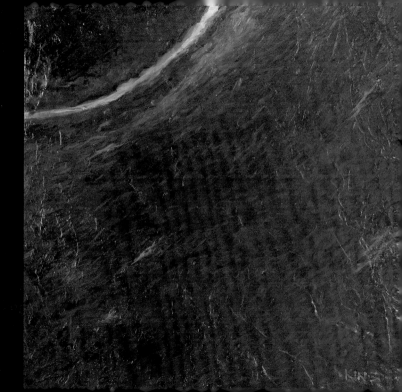

Ebb and Flow

My panel is not representational like many of the panels will most likely be.
I went for the more abstract route to express more than just one idea.
To me it represents three things that are west coast.
1) Ocean waves from a birds eye view
2) A salmon run up the coast
3) The scales of a sockeye salmon

201

Artist: Michael King, www.michaelking.ca
Panel #201
Title: Ebb and Flow
Medium: Acrylic

Forest Magic

John Muir stated, "the quickest way into the universe is through a forest wilderness." I find this to be true. Whenever I am lacking in energy or feeling "at odds" with life, I go for a walk in the woods. The effect is magical. Life becomes simple. What's important becomes clear.

202

Artist: Corinne Orazietti, www.islandspiritartworks.com
Panel #202
Title: Forest Magic
Medium: Acrylic

Melissa Goode

Panel #203   by Melissa Cole

Salmon Swirl

Although I have been diving all over the world for 18 years, one of my favorite dives is with the sockeye salmon in the cold, clear waters of the Adams River in BC.

It was otherworldly to have a mass of red salmon swirling around me. For me, these fish and their amazing lifecycle and struggle to succeed embodies the spirit of the Pacific Northwest.

203

Artist: Melissa Cole, www.melissacole.comm
Panel #203
Title: Salmon Swirl
Medium: Acrylic

E. McClelland

Wrecking Ball: Glass Sponge Reef

Glass Sponge Reefs were known only as immense Cretaceous era fossil formations over 40 million years old, until living reefs were discovered recently in B.C. These fragile, complex formations show higher fish production levels than the surrounding waters by creating valuable habitat, concentrating nutrients, and protecting nurseries of juveniles, including rockfish, flat fish, lingcod, octopus, crab and shrimp. Growing slowly for 9,000 years, now these reefs are threatened by fishery trap lines, trawl nets and down-rigger "cannonball" weights. Their silica crystal skeletons, covered by thin living tissue, are torn apart or pulled up as by-catch. Protect these reefs!

204

http://www.cpawsbc.org/campaigns/marine/glasssspongereefs.php
http://gsc.nrcan.gc.ca/marine/sponge/index_e.php

Artist: Elisabeth McClelland
Panel #204
Title: Wrecking Ball: Glass Sponge Reef
Medium: Acrylic

Chrome Island Lighthouse

Chrome Island Lighthouse is one of BC's 27 lighthouses. It is located just off the southern tip of Denman Island in the Strait of Georgia and about a mile east of Vancouver Island near Deep Bay. Lighthouses are an authentic West Coast landmark and tourist attraction; and the lightkeepers' stories are rich in marine history and lore.

205

Artist: Fay St. Marie, www.faystmarie.ca
Panel #205
Title: Chrome Island Lighthouse
Medium: Acrylic

Still Light

Two things about the West Coast of Canada constantly amaze and inspire -
the quality of light and the abundance of water any every physical state.
From my home on Bowen Island, I live within walking distance of two
lakes. The stillness and completeness of first morning light require no words

206

Artist: Janet Esseiva, www.janetesseiva.com
Panel #206
Title: Still Light
Medium: Acrylic

Panel #207   by Barry Cote

Rock Cod

207

Artist: Barry Cote, www.invisiblesun.ca
Panel #207
Title: Rock Cod
Medium: Acrylic

Panel #208 by Claude de Gaspé Alleyn

untitled

208

Artist: Claude de Gaspé Alleyn   http://perso.b2b2c.ca/claudealleyn
Panel #208
Title: untitled
Medium: Acrylic

West Coast

209

Artist: Bente Hanson, www.bentecreates.com
Panel #209
Title: Oil
Medium: Acrylic

Panel #210   by Marlene Nelmes

Northern Beauty

Lynxes are usually solitary and this one was spotted alone on Christmas Day near Rosswood, a small community north of Terrace B.C.

210

Artist: Marlene Nelmes, www.heavenlydeals.com
Panel #210
Title: Northern Beauty
Medium: Acrylic

Heather McRae

Voyage

211

Artist: Heather McRae
Panel #211
Title: Voyage
Medium: Acrylic

Panel #212   by Marc LaCaille

Octopus's Garden

212

Artist: Marc LaCaille, www.artincanada.com/marclacaille/index.html
Panel #212
Title: Octopus's Garden
Medium: Acrylic

Panel #213 by Tom Omidi

Field 213

213

Artist: Tom Omidi, www.omidigallery.com
Panel #213
Title: Field 213
Medium: Acrylic

Panel #214 by Janice Oakley

Bright Stars

214

Artist: Janice Oakley
Panel #214
Title: Bright Stars
Medium: mosaic

Through Starry Eyes

Through Starry Eyes, 1996 – Robert Davidson
Haida mask - cedar, cedar bark, horsehair, acrylic paint, silver.
With its dramatic land and sea forms, Haida-Gwaii – the Queen Charlotte Islands, to some – has influenced the Haida's world view and artistic expression since time immemorial. The Haida developed their unique formline art there five centuries ago and has seen an extraordinary renaissance in the last half century.

215

Artist: Douglas McElligott
Panel #215
Title: Through Starry Eyes, 1996 – Robert Davidson
Medium: Acrylic

Descent

216

Artist: Carl Shinkaruk, www.artincanada.com/carlshinkaruk/index.
Panel #216
Title: Descent
Medium: Acrylic

Panel #217   by Barry Tate

The Guardian

217

Artist: Barry Tate, www.barrytate.com
Panel #217
Title: The Guardian
Medium: Acrylic

Octopus

I have a soft spot for octopi, I encounter them occasionally while diving and am always amazed at their intelligence and fluidity of movement. I cringe at the thought of eating these shy creatures or worse being chopped up for crab bait as is common practice in our waters. The mural panel I was asked to complete had a lot of red and it felt natural to use this as an excuse to paint my favourite marine animal.

218

Artist: Mark Hobson, www.markhobson.com
Panel #218
Title: Octopus
Medium: Acrylic

Panel #219   by Laura Levitsky

Harbor Seals

Harbor seals are very abundant in the West Coast. While strolling along the inner harbors around the West Coast you may see a harbor seal rise from the water and look around with their large round eyes. Although they are curious, they are shy animals and prefer quiet areas and can be seen resting on uncovered sandbars, rocks and beaches when the tide is low. Although they appear quite uncoordinated on land, they are very graceful swimmers and can dive to depths exceeding 600 ft. and stay underwater up to 28 minutes.

219

Artist: Laura Levitsky, www.levitskyart.com
Panel #219
Title: Harbor Seals
Medium: Acrylic

Panel #220 by Dara Allison Harvey

Night Of The Frogs

220

Artist: Dara Allison Harvey, http://web.me.com/darallison
Panel #220
Title: Night Of The Frogs
Medium: Acrylic

Panel #221   by Ron Finnen

untitled

221

Artist: Ron Finnen, www.islandillustrators.org/illustrators/finnen.asp?p=1&img=1
Panel #221
Title: untitled
Medium: Acrylic

The Last Remaining Salmon

222

Artist: Jade Boyd, www.jadeboyd.com
Panel #222
Title: The Last Remaining Salmon
Medium: Acrylic

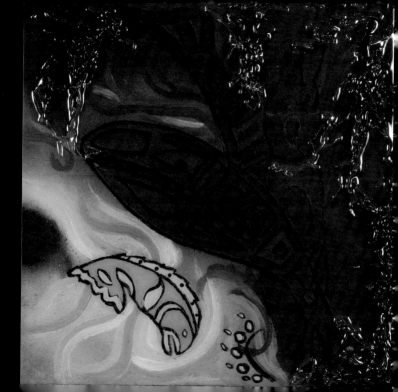

Native Soul

Our heritage, the native heritage, has a soul which is connected to nature in such a profound and subtle way...May it lead us to reconnect ourselves with the essential things in life...

223

Artist: Christine Poulin, www.christinepoulin.com
Panel #223
Title: Native Soul
Medium: Acrylic

J.Pearson

Panel #224   by Julia Pearson

There's One In Every Crowd

224

Artist: Julia Pearson
Panel #224
Title: There's One In Every Crowd
Medium: Acrylic

CStengl '04

Red Irish Lord

When I was scuba diving and spotted a red irish lord fish it felt like finding a bright jewel. Their colours and character are so striking!

225

Artist: Caroline Stengl, www.carolinestengl.com
Panel #225
Title: Red Irish Lord
Medium: Acrylic

Panel #226   by Glenna Evans

untitled (molecular Semi-abstraction)

Untitled (Molecular Semi–Abstraction) is in semblance with my series I'm currently working on at Emily Carr University of Art and Design, in 3rd year. I grew up on the west coast in the Esquimalt Harbour on Vancouver Island. When the opportunity to participate in the creation of Kunamokst arose, the memory of the infinite detail in sea life came to mind that I spent days staring at on the ocean.

226

Artist: Glenna Evans, www.glennaevans.ca
Panel #226
Title: untitled (molecular Semi-abstraction)
Medium: Oil

Denise Jones

A Sea Otters Dream World

Milo, the now famous sea otter from the Vancouver Aquarium, as I see him in his own ocean dreamworld near the Point Atkinson Lighthouse.

227

Artist: Denise Jones, www.myartclub.com/artist.php?xyz=1482
Panel #227
Title: A Sea Otters Dream World
Medium: Water Based Oils

Foreman

Adams River Sockeye

The Adams River sockeye run occurring in October is one of the largest in the world. In dominant years, over 3.5 million sockeye can return to spawn in the pristine gravel habitat of the Adams River and numerous tributaries flowing into Adams Lake.

228

Artist: Margaret Foreman, http://art.margaretforeman.com
Panel #228
Title: Adams River Sockeye
Medium: Acrylic

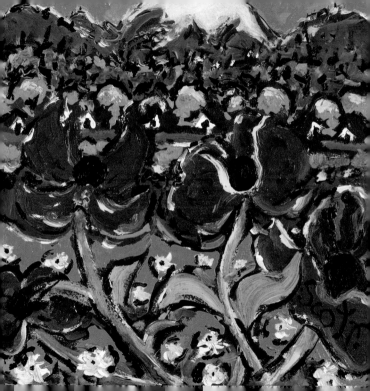

Panel #229   by Brian Scott

Comox Glacier Poppy

229

Artist: Brian Scott, www.brianscottfineart.com
Panel #229
Title: Comox Glacier Poppy
Medium: Acrylic

Galiano Oceanfront Inn and Spa

The Galiano Oceanfront Inn and Spa has been operating as a special place to stay on Galiano Island since the early part of the last century. Standing proudly in its choice waterfront location, it has long been a prominent island landmark - the first place arriving guests and islanders see when they approach by ferry. www.galianoinn.com

230

Artist: Lewis Lavoie, www.lavoiestudios.com
Panel #230
Title: Galiano Oceanfront Inn and Spa
Medium: Acrylic

Panel #231   by Lewis Lavoie

Peter's Crab

231

Artist: Lewis Lavoie, www.lavoiestudios.com
Panel #231
Title: Peter's Crab
Medium: Acrylic

Building your own Mural Mosaic

with this book
What you will need:

- Mural Mosaic pocket book
  - (the book you are holding)
- at least 44" x 84" wall space or board
- art knife & steel ruler or scissors
- adhesive (glue sticks, spray glue...)
  - straight edge, tape measure

It's EASY...

GO TO www.muralmosaic.com

- VIDEO TUTORIALS
- CLASSROOM TIPS
- MURAL BUILDERS GALLERY

Instructions

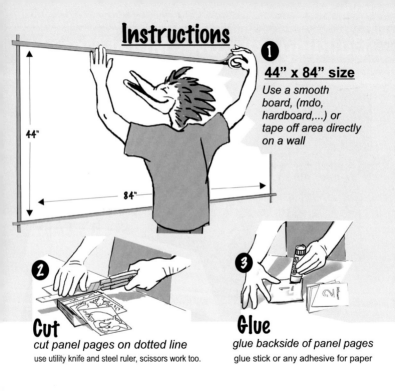

1 **44" x 84" size**

Use a smooth board, (mdo, hardboard,...) or tape off area directly on a wall

44"

84"

2 **Cut**
cut panel pages on dotted line
use utility knife and steel ruler, scissors work too.

3 **Glue**
glue backside of panel pages
glue stick or any adhesive for paper